Participating in
God's Mission
of Reconciliation

Participating in God's Mission of Reconciliation

A Resource
for Churches
in Situations
of Conflict

A Faith and Order Study Document

Faith and Order Paper 201

World Council of Churches, Geneva

Cover design: Rob Lucas

ISBN: 2-8254-1471-9

© 2006 World Council of Churches
150 route de Ferney, P.O. Box 2100
1211 Geneva 2, Switzerland
Website: http://www.wcc-coe.org

Printed in France by Lussaud

Table of Contents

I. Introduction

1. As Christians we belong to Christ. With all other Christians we share a primal baptismal identity as members of the one body of Christ. And yet this is not our only belonging; each of us is citizen of a nation, a member of an ethnic group, a speaker of a mother tongue. The churches are one in their common Lord; and yet particular churches may be identified with a nation, or associated historically and culturally with a specific ethnic, linguistic or other group. The challenge is to express such identifications and associations, in ways that do not become divisive and contradict God's gift of unity.

2. The partial and limited identities such as nation, ethnicity or language bind us with others like ourselves, bringing security and a stable cultural base upon which to build our lives. But history teaches us that, like other human characteristics, such identities can be abused, becoming idolatrous and serving as an excuse to fear, exclude and disadvantage others.

3. Where there is tension and conflict the churches are called to be bearers of Christ's presence, to be agents of reconciliation and justice. Sometimes, however, churches are so closely identified with particular groups, institutions, nations and their interests that they cannot play this reconciling role, and indeed may make conflicts worse by legitimising and promoting the interests of one party over others. When divisions among the churches reflect and reinforce divisions in society the results are often destructive, even deadly.

4. This study[1] invites the churches to examine and explore together the part they are playing in situations of tension or conflict in which ethnic and national identities are an important factor. The goals of the study are:

---

[1] The study on "Ethnic Identity, National Identity, and the Search for the Unity of the Church" has been conducted by the Faith and Order Commission of the World Council of Churches, in interaction with the WCC's Justice, Peace and Creation team.

1. To enable the churches to understand the role of ethnic and national identity in their own lives, in their relationships as churches and in their societies;

2. To renew the churches through a continuing search to manifest God's gift of unity in ways

   a) which challenge any relationship between Christian faith and ethnic or national identity that prevents unity, causes disunity, and hinders the healing of historic divisions; and

   b) which call them to transcend their divisions and the fragmentation of their societies;

3. To equip the churches to become an effective prophetic sign of the unity and renewal of a renewed human community;

4. To help the churches act as agents of reconciliation in local situations of tension and conflict.

5. While the study is addressed in the first instance to churches in situations of tension and overt conflict, nevertheless every church could benefit from a fresh look at the issues which it raises. How does our baptismal unity in Christ relate to the present divisions among the churches? How does our common belonging to Christ relate to the links, for good or ill, between churches and particular human communities and institutions? How can churches in situations of tension or conflict work together to promote reconciliation, justice and healing? These questions go to the heart of our faith, and our understanding of the nature of the church.

6. A church or a local congregation may wish to begin the study process on its own; but as soon as practicable *the process should be undertaken by the churches ecumenically*. The process itself will be an expression

of the churches' mutual accountability to one another, and to their common Lord who has set them, together, to witness in that place.

7. This study document was prepared as a resource for churches and local congregations to use in planning and carrying out such ecumenical self-study processes. The method used in the international study process is described in section II, and section III then reviews the results from four self-studies conducted locally. In sections IV, V and VI perceptions from the social sciences, biblical studies, and theology respectively are brought to bear on issues of ethnic identity, national identity, and Christian unity. Section VII urges churches in situations of tension and conflict where ethnic and national identities are major factors, to participate together in God's mission of reconciliation.

8. Section VIII extends "An Invitation to the Churches", suggesting to them a process of joint study and action involving three stages: analysing the local situation, identifying sources of conflict, and reflecting and acting together to help bring about healing and a just reconciliation. The first stage uses the set of questions described in §10, and given in full in §§17 and 178. Other questions are given at points throughout this study document, to help focus reflection on the topics under discussion at that point.

II. How the Study was Carried Out

9. The initial meeting at Hawarden in Wales (1997) on "Ethnic Identity, National Identity and the Unity of the Church" determined the methodology to be used in the study process. Two aspects emerged:

1. the witness from churches, councils of churches, and ecumenical study centres reflecting on these issues in their own local situation;

2. interdisciplinary work on ethnic identity and national

identity in relation to Christian unity, drawing specifically
on the resources of biblical studies, theology, church
history, and the social sciences.

Both aspects were, from the outset, to be fully integrated.

A. Local self-studies

10. A series of local self-studies, organized by councils of churches or
other kinds of church-related bodies, were supported by Faith and
Order. These were conducted ecumenically by churches and
Christians who found themselves involved in ethnic or national conflicts. The study processes, means of reporting and results varied
according to local circumstances; but all the processes were asked to
address a common set of questions.[2] This allowed each study to
analyse its local situation in its own terms, while providing a common
basis for discussion and reflection among the studies, and between the
studies and biblical scholars, theologians and social scientists.

11. Local self-study projects were supported in Fiji, Sudan, Northern
Ireland, Sri Lanka, and the USA. These were varied in nature and
scope, depending on the local situation; some clearly involved an
interfaith dimension, others have sought to address the issue of racial
identity.

B. Interdisciplinary work

12. The key themes which were emerging, were to be explored
through the interaction of biblical scholars, church historians, theologians and social scientists. Two areas of exploration emerged: the first
involved the biblical witness, whilst the second concerned the categories of ethnicity, nationalism and race. These were approached as
follows:

---

[2] See §§ 17 and 178.

1. The biblical witness: a group of biblical scholars came together to share their work. They had been given the freedom to choose their own biblical texts and topics. Two clear groupings emerged:

   a) The Enemy, Alienation and Reconciliation,
   b) Building Identities, Belonging and Salvation.

2. Clarification of terminology: a group of social scientists and theologians sought to clarify the relationships between ethnic and national identities and race, nation and state, church and state together with theological reflections on the place of these terms in God's creation and redemption.

C. Integration

13. The final stage of the study programme brought together the local self-studies, the reflections of biblical scholars, and the reflections of theologians and social scientists, allowing these three streams to interact with one another. The present document is the result of that process of interaction and integration.

III. Situations of Conflict

A. A mission of reconciliation and unity

14. In situations of conflict the church, as part of the new creation, is entrusted with a mission for unity exercised not least through a ministry of reconciliation. Such a ministry presupposes, on the one hand, our witness to the "other" about God in Christ and, on the other, our openness to allow God to speak to us through the "other". Mission, when understood in this light, has no room for triumphalism; it contributes to removing the causes of religious animosity and the violence that often goes with it.

15. The religious traditions of humankind, in their great diversity, are "journeys" or "pilgrimages" towards human fulfilment and a search for the truth about human existence. Even though human beings may be strangers to each other, there are moments when their paths intersect that call for the exercise of "hospitality". Both personal experiences today, and historical moments in the past, witness to the fact that such hospitality is possible and does take place.

B. Local self-studies

16. Four major self-studies were engaged in ecumenically by churches in situations of tension and conflict, where the deepest divisions among persons and churches were centred around issues of ethnic and national identities. Local self-studies completed in Fiji[3] and the Sudan[4], and material made available from on-going local study processes in Sri Lanka and Northern Ireland, have been used in this text. Local study processes are still under consideration in Wales, the USA and South Africa.

17. As noted in §10, a common set of questions was addressed to each of the local self-studies. These questions were as follows (they are repeated in §178 of section VIII, the "Invitation to the churches").

1. What churches are present in your situation? What is their relationship to the various parties in tension or conflict? What is their relationship to each other, and to church or other bodies overseas?

2. How far do the divisions (both confessional and social) within – and among – the churches reflect divisions within society as a whole?

---

[3] See *Ethnicity, National Identity & Church Unity: A Study on Fiji 2001, Commissioned by Faith and Order; World Council of Churches*, Suva, Citizens' Constitutional Forum, 2004.

[4] See "Ethnic Identity, National Identity and Unity of the Church in the Sudan", Khartoum, Sudan Council of Churches, November, 2001.

3. How do the churches understand, and address, issues of ethnic and national identity in your situation?

4. What do the churches understand to be their mission in your situation?

5. Upon what resources in Christian tradition do the churches draw in order to interpret - and offer hope within - your situation?

6. What external resources have the churches brought to bear on the situation?

7. How has the churches' engagement helped to effect change in your local situation?

8. What specific lessons have been learned about how the churches can help reduce tension and conflict, and promote a just peace, in your own context?

9. What have the churches learned from their engagement in this process about the unity of the church?

1. Ireland

18. Ireland's population is 4 million
Religion: 92% are Roman Catholic, 3% are Church of Ireland [Anglican]

Northern Ireland's population is 1.7 million
Religion: 56% are Protestant, 41% are Roman Catholic.

"The struggle for power between Unionist, British Protestants and Republican, Irish Catholics lies at the heart of this long-standing conflict".

Ireland was able to assimilate into its culture many of its immigrants, notably the Normans. In the seventeenth century large numbers of English and Scottish Protestants were planted[5] in Ulster and were never assimilated - probably because they were Protestants. What had been an Irish/English divide became also a Catholic/Protestant divide. These national communities were and are distinguished by their allegiance to differing Christian traditions, and not by language. So Protestant churches are politically Unionist and British, whilst Roman Catholics are both nationalist and Irish.

19. One of the working hypotheses and tentative conclusions made by the local self-study group in Northern Ireland was the depressing failure of the churches to make a difference to the ongoing conflicts. Ecumenical activity has survived in the province; but, whilst this is remarkable, it does not include some of the larger Protestant churches.

20. In almost four hundred years, politico-religious conflict has never gone away and at times has turned into extreme violence. The two communities are bitterly divided along Protestant-Catholic lines; these are, when combined with ethno-national and politico-religious divisions, a recipe for conflict. In Northern Ireland the Protestants held all the levers of power, and in consequence Catholics consistently experienced discrimination and marginalisation; whilst in the south in Ireland, Protestants are occasionally reminded that a state with a Catholic-majority would not always be welcoming.

21. During the past two centuries, movements that attempted to cross this ethno-national and politico-religious divide – a divide principally based on class or economic considerations – have largely failed. Such failures show the strength of the divide.

2. Fiji

22. In addressing its own situation, the local self-study in Fiji paid par-

---

[5] In the 17th century a significant number of poor farmers in England, and Scotland in particular, were moved to plantations in the north of Ireland.

ticular attention to the common study questions which were provided.[6]

23. The population of Fiji is 880,000.
    Ethnicity: 51% Fijian, 44% Indian (Indo-Fijian)
    Religion: 52% Christian (Meth: 37%), 38% Hindu, 8% Muslim.

The multi-ethnic composition of Fijian society more or less parallels
its religious diversity. Indigenous Fijians and others are mostly
Christians, while Indo-Fijians are largely Hindus and Muslims.

> *"Upon the election of an Indo-Fijian as Prime Minister the*
> *Fijian police staged a coup, which was the spark that ignited the*
> *present conflict".*

24. The churches' reconciliatory role can be seen in two interrelated
contexts: first, the need to manifest unity within and between the
churches themselves; and secondly, the churches' wider role in working towards national reconciliation. Because the church is one of the
most important institutions in Fiji, Christian unity has implications for
national reconciliation. However, the Christian churches in Fiji are far
from being ideologically or politically monolithic. Various church
groups are entangled in ethnic politics, whilst national politics have
permeated some church politics.

25. In this regard Christianity has become an ideological force which
underpins ethno-nationalism, with its demands for the paramountcy[7]
of Fijian interests. One of the features of the paramountcy of Fijian
interests is seen in religious domination and persecution (e.g. Sunday
road blocks and the fire-bombing of Hindu temples). In order to
achieve national unity, the government's intention is for everyone to
become a Christian. The fundamentalist faction within the majority
Methodist church espouses the revival of the concept of the Christian

---

[6] See *Ethnicity, National Identity & Church Unity: A Study on Fiji 2001*, pp. 60-65.
[7] This is the term preferred in the discussion in Fiji; it indicates the condition of being
superior to all other interests and groups.

state. The issue of national identity, as such, is not addressed because once Fiji becomes a Christian state the *Lotu* (the church) will be one of the ingredients that contributes to national identity.

3. Sudan

26. The population of the Sudan is 39 million.
     Ethnicity: 52% are black, 39% Arab & 6% Beja (northern nomads).
     Religion: 70% Muslim (Sunni), 25% Indigenous beliefs & 5% Christian.

It is estimated that there are 570 tribes in Sudan; these have been gathered into 56 ethnic groups in terms of their linguistic, cultural and other ethnological characteristics. The south and the north reveal great differences in ethnic composition. In the north, Islam and Arabic have influenced the culture, although the population is still divided into Arabs and non-Arabs on the basis of ethnicity, language and social modes of life.

> *"The aim of the Sudanese government to impose its rule and culture on the southern region of the country has provoked the present conflict".*

27. In Southern Sudan the major ethnic groups differ, not only in their languages and culture, but also in their population sizes and the geographical areas they occupy. Land occupied by a group is defended as territory which sustains that group's livelihood. There is overwhelming evidence showing that ethnic groups have moved in search of better land; as a result some ethnic groups have gained, whilst others have lost their land in the process.

28. Despite all these differences in ethnic groupings, and diverse as they are, the power elite in Khartoum perceives Sudan as a geographical space where everyone must be converted to Islam, and adopt Islamic values, before national unity can be achieved. Consequently

the national identity of the Sudan is not conceived in multicultural and pluralistic terms. The ideal national identity, according to those in power, is Islam.

29. The majority of Christians are found in Southern Sudan. Social and economic policies discriminate against Christians. Christian private schools and health services, in the main, benefit rich Muslim families. Christians have dominated the trade and service sector in Khartoum and other urban communities, but the policy of the Muslim-dominated government has targeted them in order to Islamise the market.

4. Sri Lanka

30. The population of Sri Lanka is 20 million.
    Ethnicity: 74% Sinhalese, 18% Tamil, 7% Moor
    Religion: 70% Buddhist, 15% Hindu, 8% Christian & 7% Muslim.

Sri Lanka, once known as Ceylon, achieved independence as a dominion within the British Commonwealth in 1948. The government adopted socialist policies, strengthening social services and maintained a strong economy, but at the same time disenfranchised 800,000 Tamil plantation workers. The Sinhalese nationalist Solomon Bandaranaike was elected Prime Minister in 1956 and drove a "Sinhala Only" law through parliament, making Sinhalese the national language and, as a result, reserving the best jobs for the Sinhalese. The political aim was to address the imbalance of power between the majority Sinhalese and the minority English-speaking Christians, the educated elite. But at the same time it enraged the Tamil Hindu minority who began to press for a federal system of government - which would give the main Tamil areas in the north and east, greater autonomy.

31. The country's ethnic tensions and religious conflicts began and have since escalated, as competition for wealth and work has intensified. Sinhalese and Tamils are both guilty of intimidation and massacres, now known as "ethnic cleansing". The Sri Lankan government

has oscillated between political solutions and military offensives, neither of which has ended massacres and terrorism.

32. In 1972 the constitution formally made Buddhism the state's primary religion; one effect was the reduction of university places for Tamils. Subsequent civil unrest resulted in a state of emergency in Tamil areas. In consequence, many Tamils moved north into Tamil-dominated areas whilst Sinhalese began to leave the Jaffna area. Since the outbreak of hostilities in the 1980s between the Government and Tamil separatists, several hundred thousand civilians have fled the country.

33. The local self-study group has suggested that the churches in Sri Lanka have not adequately addressed issues of ethnic identity, nor matters of violence and issues of power related to devolution. Further, they suggest that this was the way in which the churches have avoided allowing conflicts to surface within their congregations.

34. The various Christian denominations have neither a common stand nor a common plan of action. Denominationalism rather than Christian unity appears to have triumphed.

35. Several issues still need to be examined. Amongst these are accusations levelled against the churches that they are "pro-Tamil". Further, the churches are accused of indirectly advocating - and even causing - the conflict in order to make converts. Even if these accusations have no basis in fact, the allegations are deeply rooted, especially amongst the extremist Sinhalese.

C. Signs of hope

36. The analyses from these four local self-studies do not give the whole picture, since even in the short time since the studies were undertaken the situation has changed in some respects. In Fiji, for example, the need for inter-religious dialogue has been recognized and

undertaken on an ecumenical basis. These dialogues have resulted in the creation of an inter-religious council on which the religious leaders sit, and so ensure continuing communication and relationships should further conflict emerge.

37. In the Sudan, the Christian South was divided as various tribal factions, associated with particular denominations, were able to have neither a common goal nor a common strategy. The World Council of Churches provided a safe ecumenical space at a meeting in Morges, Switzerland, in which the process towards making unity visible was pursued as a step towards resolution of tribal conflicts in the South. At the time of writing this study document (Spring, 2005) peace initiatives have been undertaken by the Khartoum government.

38. Ireland has seen a growing ecumenical co-operation between Roman Catholics and many of the churches of the Reformation. Whilst as noted this does not include all the Protestant churches, these ecumenical developments have undergirded many community initiatives, showing that the visible unity of the church plays an important role in the resolution of conflict. As is shown in Section VI on Theological Perceptions, the "Reconciliation of Memories" (§§145-153) has played a key role in addressing the issues in many of the border villages where communities are particularly divided.

D. Common features found in these studies

39. Several features are common to the situations of conflict explored in the various local self-studies. These include the following:

1. Discriminatory practices based upon ethnic or inter-confessional grounds have caused conflict.

2. Ideological differences to be found within ethnic or religious communities have caused conflict between - and within - them.

3. Religious and ethnic divisions have been be intertwined, intensifying existing conflicts.[8]

4. The combination of a nation state with a single religious tradition has caused conflict.

IV. Perceptions from the Social Sciences

A. Human identity and community

40. Christian churches are united in their belief that baptism constitutes the primary identity of each of their members (see §§1, 114-118). This study is based on the theological conviction that the identity which Christians receive through baptism is their overarching identity, under which are subsumed all the other identities (gender, race, cultural, ethnic, political or class) which people inherit, assume and develop in history.

41. Human beings are made in, by, and for community. This is a human characteristic which finds expression in many forms and under many names. Such identities are socially "constructed", and grow out of a basic human need for relationship and community. As such they are, in origin and essence, positive and benign or, at the very least, neutral. However, when identities are misused, distorted, or manipulated - and especially when they are turned against the "other" - they become destructive. Indeed, it sometimes seems that mention of ethnicity, nationalism, tribalism or racism is only made in reference to situations of conflict.

B. The contribution of the social sciences

42. In order to help the churches analyse effectively situations in which human groupings or communities initiate or exacerbate con-

---

[8] For example in Sri Lanka: Buddhist/Sinhalese and Hindu, Christian/Tamil; in the Sudan, the Christian south of the country and the Muslim north.

flict, the study process called upon a number of social scientists. Their insights are reported in order to help the churches understand the role of human groupings in making the unity of the church visible; to make responsible choices in situations of conflict; to provide an instrument by which the churches may discern whether or not the choices they have made, and the actions they have taken, have contributed to oppressive and unjust living conditions. Social analysis can assist the churches to perceive unintended, even tacit negative factors that - despite their commitment to God's mission of reconciliation - have influenced their actions.

43. Definitions used by social scientists for ethnicity, nation, tribe and race vary significantly; those that are used in this study are fairly standard. In particular contexts, however, these terms might be defined in other ways. Reflecting on the contributions made by participants representing various local self-studies (from Fiji, Northern Ireland, Sri Lanka, the USA), it is clear that all such concepts and definitions need to be contextualised. That is, what has proved helpful is not working from abstract definitions, but rather analysing how various markers of identity and difference "work" within each specific context.

C. Tools for analysis

1. Ethnicity and nationalism

44. Ethnicity, nation, tribe and (to a degree) race, can be overlapping forms of identity. Their similarity is suggested by the way in which some scholars have adopted the term "ethno-national". However, there are distinctions to be made. *Ethnicity* involves a degree of common culture, often including one or more of the following markers in common: physical characteristics, language, origin, historical experience and religion. In many current situations, ethnicity is associated with minority status; immigrants, in particular, are often perceived as ethnic groups. A *nation* in the strict sense, often referred to as a "national group", shares many of the characteristics of ethnicity, but has a tendency to be culturally more self-conscious and politically

assertive. As such, they regard self-rule as a legitimate right and, as will be seen, such political aspirations of national groups are fulfilled by their functioning as a *modern state*. By this definition, "nations" have existed in many times and places.

45. Ethnic and national groups may believe themselves to be "natural" – belonging in some way to the order of nature - and fixed in form. But in fact all such groups are (whether consciously or unconsciously) "constructed", in the sense that they result from the interplay of historical and cultural factors. Such identities are therefore fluid, constantly being "renegotiated". Because these changes often result from interaction with other groups, ethnic identities are never pure; they involve multiple borrowings and adaptations, even when the sources of the changes have been lost in the mists of time.

2. Tribalism

46. Like race, the language of tribe is difficult to use and requires careful analysis. There are times when its characteristics spill over into groups which can be defined, as ethnic or national. Before defining the term, it needs to be emphasised that "tribe" and "tribal" are neutral sociological categories, whereas "tribalism" is a pathological, destructive state of religious, cultural and ethnic absolutism. It emerges when a particular tribal identity is vested with power to subdue and surmount all other identities. Tribalism becomes enormously destructive when a tribe seeks to identify with, or seize control of, the state as a vehicle for enforcing its pattern of identity over all other forms. This often results in extreme discrimination and the denial of human rights.

47. For the purposes of this study a *tribe* is a nexus of blood, historical and cultural roots, associated with a common land which stimulates and helps generate a tribal identity (a classic example is the twelve tribes of Israel, each of whom claim descent from a common ancestor). Tribes tend to be exclusive, setting clear boundaries outside

which exists "the other" (whereas many nations, for example, have permeable boundaries). Examples of the existence of tribes are to be found many modern African states, not least in Rwanda, but also in the post-colonial state of Zimbabwe. In the Pacific islands, similar tribal identities are associated with particular islands or clans, making up modern or post-colonial nation states.

3. Racism

48. Often more pertinent and persuasive as dividing lines between different groups, are racist attitudes held by a group which sees itself as superior to others. *Race* is constructed on the basis of perceived shared external features, for example skin colour. This construction has had momentous historical consequences. For example, the justification, legitimisation, and rationalisation of the European colonial conquest in the 18th and 19th centuries went hand in hand with racism: claiming superiority, the colonisers took for themselves the right to oppress and exploit others. Their anthropology was aimed at demonstrating the inferiority of the peoples being colonised and enslaved, as well as at devaluing their culture, religion and social organization. The claim to alleged white superiority continues to be at the root of the most pertinent forms of racism today - although racism can, and does, surface in the relationships and conflicts between other groups.

49. The factors of race, ethnicity and nation are related in different ways in different contexts. Sometimes race coincides with ethnicity or nation, so that all members of the given ethnic or national group share the same racial features. Where ethnicity or nation is the dominant identity, race may be a subcategory: the Brazilian nation, with its many racial differences, is a good example. In other cases, however, a nation or state may be fundamentally divided along racial lines, with ethnicity a sub-category. Here the United States, with its pervasive white-black division, is a striking example, with both racial categories subsuming significant ethnic diversity.

50. This study seeks to address conflict based on ethnic, national, and racial identities. Regrettably groups based on these identities - even when they have lived in peace alongside, or among, one other for a long time and with no memory of destructive conflict - can turn upon each other with devastating consequences. Sometimes this results from a threat, whether perceived or real: perhaps competition for a scarce resource; perhaps from a sense that another group is prospering at the expense of one's own, or even threatening its existence; perhaps from a new awareness that behind the issues of ethnic or national identity may lie fundamental socio-economic injustices which also need to be addressed.

51. In other cases, however, the threat arises not so much from the interactions between the groups concerned but from external manipulation. Thus many current ethnic and national conflicts can be traced back to divisions which surfaced in the colonial past. In the most extreme cases, this division was created by the colonial powers - a destructive possibility arising from the fact that, as noted, ethnic and national identities are "constructed". The outstanding example may be Rwanda, where European social scientists and colonial regimes defined the Hutu and Tutsi as separate peoples, where previously there had been no such consciousness. More often, however, the colonial regime manipulated existing groups, whether they had been living in peace or in conflict, by privileging some at the expense of others.

52. One may well ask, Why should people attach importance to their ethnic identities? One of the oldest explanations is that people "have been that way" from time immemorial, they have "always" been defined by their origins, language, custom, religion, race, territory, and destiny. Ethnicity is deeply rooted in human consciousness and primordially defines peoples' being in the world, so much so that conflict, at some time or another, is more than likely when a country is inhabited by more than one ethnic group. (This primordial understanding of ethnicity, despite its popular acceptance, cannot account for the complexities of ethnic consciousness. It cannot explain how

such consciousness is formed, how it changes over time, why it varies in intensity among people of the same group, and why people build and defend relationships that cut across ethnic boundaries. Nevertheless the fact remains that many people do attach great importance to their ethnic identity.)

53. The following questions are provided for use by the churches in analysing their own situation. These may help clarify how the terms discussed in §§44-52 apply – or do not apply – to particular local contexts.

Ethnicity

- Can you distinguish various ethnic groups in your context?
- What characteristics define each as an ethnic group? (Physical characteristics, shared language, religion etc. - See §44)

Nationalism

- Can you distinguish national groups, as opposed to ethnic groups in your context?
- What characteristics define each as a national group? (See §44)
- What political aspirations does each national group hold?

Tribe

- Can you distinguish various tribes in your context?
- What characteristics define the membership of these tribes?
- Does one tribe control the levers of power in your situation?

Racism

- Can you perceive racist attitudes within your
  context?
- Does one ethnic or national group perceive itself
  superior to others?
- Is race a primary identity, embodying within it ethnic
  and national identities?

4. The nation-state

54. As noted in §44, "nation" is understood to include peoples with
some shared cultural and other identity markers, as well as a sense of
common destiny. The "nation-state" adds to this the political systems
and administrative structures necessary for the nation to function as a
sovereign entity.

55. While nation-states have existed in many places and at many times,
because of its relevance to the present world situation the study has
focused on the *modern nation-state* as it emerged in Europe over several centuries. It is commonly argued that the modern nation-state arose
in continental Europe at the time of the French Revolution. A
Napoleonic model of state administration was most often preferred;
but in some cases, for instance in the United Kingdom, the origins of
the nation-state lie in the first millennium. For others in 19th century
Europe, the process of industrialisation and subsequent urbanisation
established a tight correspondence between the state and the nation.
Its relevance for the present situation lies in the fact that it was this
modern nation state that was imposed on many parts of the world
through the European "colonial project" of the 19th century. It has
now become an essential building block for the post-World War II
international political system.

56. It should be obvious, but is not, that the "nation-state" embraces
the totality of the peoples which it incorporates and not just those
who determine the political process. The nation-state has a responsi-

bility to protect the rights of minorities and the weaker sections of society, whilst providing the necessary resources to allow them to live with dignity. In a justly-ordered nation-state there must be interaction between the people as a whole and the political "actors" in order to shape social policy and, for example, to revise legal systems and constitutions. This interaction must cut across ethnic and religious divides.

57. Social scientists make a crucial distinction between "civic" versus "ethnic" nationalism. These distinctions have important implications. There is a version of nationalism that rests fundamentally on the ideals of citizenship, and involves a commitment to common "civic" participation in accord with constitutional norms. There is a different version of nationalism that rests its aspirations for a state upon a belief in the "prior existence" of a community, one that distinguishes itself from foreigners according to its special history and culture. These two versions of nationalism indicate "tendencies" and "options" available to nations under modern conditions. There are numerous intermediate types.

58. Nation-states are formed in different ways depending on their specific context. The idea developed that a sovereign state should become a *nation* state, one that protects the common interests of people who believe they share a common culture, language and territory. It is obvious (because of size, for example) that not every group could form a state. During the period of imperial domination and clashes over territory, groups were ranked according to whether they were "a nation", "a nationality", "a national minority" or "a tribe". This classification has had a lasting impact upon the way ethnic claims are pursued in the world today. In some countries, for instance, waves of immigrants have had considerable impact on nation-building. These complex realities can become the breeding ground for conflict and violence if the state does not function as a fair intermediary between the various groups and interests in society, guaranteeing justice for the poor and protection for minorities on the basis of the economic, social, and cultural rights of all citizens.

59. To secure this protective and pro-active role of the state, a distinction must be made between national belonging (the historical or cultural identification with the nation) and citizenship (the legal status granting full access to political and social rights and responsibilities in the nation-state). Sometimes only a core population – the "nation" which forms the basis of the "nation-state" - is given full citizenship, while minorities not belonging to the "nation", in the strict sense, have only limited access to the political process and to social services. Only full citizenship for all persons within the nation-state can guarantee equal rights and equal treatment for all. The constant weakening of the role of states in the context of economic globalisation undermines the state's necessary, pro-active role in ensuring life with dignity, and in maintaining just and sustainable communities.

5. Civil society

60. Any comprehensive instrument to help the churches to analyse their own situation must include the term "civil society". This refers to the sectors of a given society which, though not part of the formal political and economic system, provide a vehicle for input into the political process. Civil society comprises many different groups with different, sometimes conflicting or contradictory interests and aims. It is, in many ways, the "arena", or "community space" in which political and ideological debate can take place in a society, the place where values and options are discussed by the broadest range of groups and interests.

61. The following questions are provided for use by the churches in analysing their own situation. These may help clarify how the terms discussed in §§54-60 apply – or do not apply – to particular local contexts.

Nation

- How did your nation-state come into being?
- In its foundation did it inherit any factors which have

       lead to community conflict?

      - Does your nation-state act in an equitable manner to all its peoples or does it give certain groups preferential treatment?

6. Church and state relationships

62. Within the first four centuries of the history of the church the relationship between tribe, nation or state, and the church emerged. In the Roman Empire the Christian church, subsequent to periods of persecution, was tolerated and even given a favoured position in the empire; eventually the church exercised considerable control over its affairs. In many areas identified as belonging to particular tribes or nations, the principle of "Whoever rules determines the religion,"[9] was followed (this principle was effective in Europe at the time of the Reformation).

63. The closeness of the relation between churches and nation-states varies widely. At one end of the spectrum is a theocracy in which the church and the state are conterminous. A less extreme position is the state church, in which the state has the duty to support and assist the church, legitimising its organisation and administration to the (more or less complete) exclusion of all other churches. At the other end of the spectrum, church and state are wholly separate. A wide variety of terms - state church, established church, state-recognized church, autocephalous church[10] - is used, and each context must be analysed carefully in order to grasp the role of the church in each particular modern nation state.

64. Where a close relationship exists between a particular church and the state, the church can find itself responsible for legitimising the exclusion of other religious traditions, the repression of minorities

---

[9] *Cuius regio, eius religio.*
[10] This term describes a "self-governing" Orthodox church, usually in predominately Orthodox regions, e.g. Cyprus.

and the denial of human rights. But such a church can also play a prophetic role, challenging the state in its actions and encouraging the application of the principle of equity to all the citizens of the state. As noted, the relationship between a church and the state can sustain or even provoke community conflict. There are examples to be found in the local self-studies from Fiji and Ireland.

7. World faith communities

65. Religion can, and should be a force for human liberation. In many areas in which there are ethnic and national conflicts, world faith communities have played an active part, sometimes for good and sometimes for ill. In analysing such conflicts the role played by faith communities needs to be determined. Where a faith community is closely identified with the state but also with a particular ethnic group, the latter could use this identification as a means to gain a dominant position in society, and to oppress other groups. In other situations, the nation state itself has espoused one particular religious tradition as a means of achieving national unity - but at a significant expense. Examples from the local self-studies of such close relationships are to be found with Islam in the Sudan and with Buddhism in Sri Lanka. Similar relationships exists between Christian confessions and nation states in Fiji (Methodism), in Ireland (Roman Catholic) and Northern Ireland (Protestant).

66. The following questions are provided for use by the churches in analysing their own situation. These may help clarify how the terms discussed in §§62-65 apply – or do not apply – to particular local contexts.

Church, faith traditions and the state:

- Has any Christian tradition an exclusive association with the state?
- Has any other faith tradition a close or exclusive association with the state?

- Does this association legitimise the policies and
  actions of the state?
- Is this association characterised by its challenge to, or
  support of, the state in ensuring equitable arrangements for all its citizens?

D. Reasons for conflict

67. After an initial analysis of their situation using some of the above
terms and concepts, churches may find it helpful to consider the genesis of local conflicts. In particular local situations, some or all of the
following may be contributing factors.

1. Colonisation

68. Some contemporary problems have arisen in and through a
region's colonial history — a history which continues to impact the
present. In pre-colonial times these territories had indigenous political systems; some of these, for example, the Inca and Aztec empires
and some African and Asian kingdoms, were at least equally developed and stable (not to mention equally oppressive) as those in the
colonisers' own countries. Yet on the way to independence many former colonial territories were forced to conform to western models of
"nation" and the "nation-state", without having the chance to work
through a range of crucial historical, social and political issues arising
in the process.

69. The political arrangements imposed on the colonies were meant
to serve the interests of the colonisers, facilitating the transfer of
wealth. The colonial enterprise often played one ethnic community
off against the other (a policy of "divide and rule"). This resulted in
the creation of "states" that are quite artificial and do not follow pre-
colonial - though still important - political and cultural contours.
Unfortunately there have been few successful attempts to find alter-
natives to inherited colonial models of nation-building: Tanzania is an

exception, having successfully integrated different ethnic and religious groups in an artificially created geographical unit.

2. Globalisation

70. If colonisation has left a legacy of inappropriate social and political systems, then the bequest of the contemporary world is economic globalisation, a compelling and comprehensive system that characterises our age. There are advantages in linking the world as one human family; but the globalisation of capital and markets generates economic disparities and erodes the values of primary communities, values which give coherence to people's lives.

71. Many people experience a new degree of uncertainty, fear of volatile and unfair economic conditions, and estrangement from established patterns of personal and social life. This has resulted in religious, cultural and ethnic absolutisms, exploding into senseless violence against the "other" (whether imagined or real), against persons or communities perceived as a threat to one's social, economic and political interests and well-being. Here religion accentuates difference, deepening solidarity among those who feel threatened and generating passion against the "adversaries". On the other hand the new uncertainty may lead to religious, cultural and ethnic fragmentation, resulting in the abandonment of local identities as globalism is accepted. In this case religion underplays difference, over-emphasising the false "good news" of the new, one-dimensional world.

3. Development

72. Despite hopes that globalisation would bring improved standards of living, many people in the developing world have seen little or no improvement in their standard of living; indeed in some countries this has deteriorated to an alarming level. Problems are also emerging in countries in the developed world, where standards of living are well above poverty levels. In Western Europe the dynamics of a globalised economy have led to high levels of unemployment; the costs of main-

taining social welfare programmes are rising faster than wealth creation; and governments are being elected on platforms of low taxation (and, by implication, low public welfare provisioning). More and more people are becoming functionally irrelevant to national economies, and find it increasingly difficult to cope under these conditions. In such situations policies of development, if they are to be sustainable, must be sensitive to problems of marginalisation, social inequalities, immigration and political instability.

73. Within the context of the general crisis associated with current approaches to development, more specific policies may be needed for countries that are divided on the basis of ethnicity and religion. Here the main issue is that of equality. Many ethnic conflicts or grievances can be traced to the way in which unequal opportunities are available to groups in the social economy, and groups experience discrimination or inequalities in accessing jobs, incomes, holding assets and receiving social services. As social inequalities widen, disadvantaged persons may become intolerant of "ethnic strangers" within their neighbourhoods. In plural but unequal societies, redistributive policies are essential in bringing about reconciliation, a sense of national belonging, and political stability.

4. Power

74. Power has been a common and central factor in the local self-studies undertaken in contexts of ethnic and national conflict. Who controls political, economic, cultural, religious and military power? Is this power shared? If so, with whom is this power shared? Is it used to empower disadvantaged groups? These have been key questions in the local self-studies relating to a range of issues: the tensions and open war between the Sinhalese majority and the Tamil minority in Sri Lanka; the war in the Sudan; the coup d'états in Fiji; and the holding of the levers of economic and political power in Northern Ireland. Each of these examples shows the destructive interplay of different forms of power.

75. But there is a deeper question: Is power really a morally neutral instrument, merely "the force by which something can be done"? Is it the motive and manner by which power is exercised that makes it prone to abuse? Is power, as Max Weber commented, the capacity to force one's will and decisions upon others?.[11]

76. Given the growing concentration of power in a few hands, both nationally and internationally, the questions asked at a national level need also to be asked in the international context: Who controls the global economy and money markets? Which communities or nations are thereby marginalised or excluded? These questions have immediate implications: in such circumstances, those who have experienced structural injustice often respond with violence.

77. One obstacle to a peaceful resolution of conflicts is often the exercise of power of interpretation. This is the power to define the "correct" understanding and representation of reality, to define the terms in which issues are discussed, to write a community's history. It is exercised locally but also globally, by those who control the media. Such power becomes problematic when it is allied to systems of domination, to social systems that produce certain kinds of knowledge of a kind that controls, alienates, subjugates, fragments and neutralises. Such distortions of knowledge prevent humanity from discerning clearly the signs of the times and distance people from truth, goodness and justice, diminishing their capacity to live life abundantly.

78. The power of interpretation plays a role in exacerbating conflicts by portraying the "other" as a threat or as "the enemy", and thus legitimising violence. The power of interpretation can either block or enable reconciliation. How a group perceives itself in relation to and

---

[11] The ecumenical critique of such a position is clear. See the Seoul Affirmation 1: "We affirm that all exercise of power is accountable to God…Therefore we affirm that all forms of human power and authority are subject to God and accountable to people. This means the right of people to full participation. In Christ, God decisively revealed the meaning of power as compassionate love that prevails over the forces of death". In *Now is the time: Final Document & Other Texts from the World Convocation on Justice, Peace and the Integrity of Creation, Seoul 1990*, WCC, 1990, p. 12.

over against others depends, to a large extent, on their respective collective memories and how these relate to one another (see "The Reconciliation of Memories", §§148-156).

E. Offering a positive response: possible roles for the churches

79. Religion can and should be a force for human liberation, but it has often been used as a force of oppression. Churches and other faith communities need to emphasise the liberative elements of their faith, and ensure that its spiritual resources are brought to the search for just and reconciled communities. In order to have an effective voice, the need for the churches to make their unity manifest becomes all the more important. At a national level churches, and other religious groups, are called to remind the state of its pro-active role in establishing a greater degree of justice, peace and protection of people's livelihoods. The churches need to take a vigilant role, raising their voice against any decisions taken by governments, or promoted by powerful interests in society, which have negative impacts on the economic, social and cultural rights of all citizens.

80. As noted, in some countries particular religious traditions have not been able to play this role because they have been so closely identified with the state, or with a particular ethnic group striving for a dominant position. Churches and other religious traditions may need to reassess their role in order to maintain a critical distance from the state and other interests active in the public sphere, if they are to play their proper role in society and to be an effective prophetic sign of the *basileia* of God.[12]

81. In summary, churches and other religious groups should be a sign of unity and solidarity in their society. At times they have failed to do

---

[12] Because of negative overtones the term "kingdom of God", whilst being widely used and known, is replaced in this study document by the term "*basileia*", used in the sense of "the reign of God".

so, to the detriment of peace and just relationships. This is all the more tragic given that churches often include members from different ethnic communities, and therefore have the opportunity – and obligation - to "model" unity and harmony among such communities.

1. Making common cause

82. Such an active stance by the churches calls for cooperation with others active in civil society, namely persons or groups who support a similar vision of life in community. Together these parties could foster the social development of marginalised groups overlooked by the state. They should also address the misuse of power, and the root causes of ethnic strife and violence.

2. Institutional change

83. To ensure that groups do not feel alienated from vital political processes shaping their lives, institutional changes may be needed. The nature and the authority of the state may need to be redefined, in light of the pluralism which now characterises so many countries and in view of the fact that global transactions in business, politics, security, culture and social affairs have undermined much of the effectiveness of the nation state. (This is not to deny the persistent feeling that the state is the ultimate symbol of a group's sense of freedom, and the foundation for its progress. This is based on the concept of "self-determination" – a sacred symbol for judging a group's maturity and civilisation, and justifying its participation in the conduct of international affairs.)

84. As noted, size and other factors mean that it is simply not possible for every group to become a nation-state. This fact calls for a fundamental rethinking of the concept of nation-state, including its underlying principle of self-determination. The changes needed to stabilise ethnic relations and reduce conflicts require a reorientation and reorganization of the state system. States may need to grant much greater autonomy, rights and freedoms to the various groups that con-

stitute the society, and the state itself may need to ensure that it embodies the varied identities of such groups in its relations, both internally and to the international community. Four key policies, each with its own risks and unique possibilities, can be identified based on the experience of countries that have tried to move in this direction: the devolution of power; power-sharing arrangements; an electoral system that seeks to reflect the pluralistic character of the population; and cultural policies that promote harmonious relations among diverse groups.

85. While constitutional lawyers and policy makers are addressing some of these institutional policy changes, the churches may contribute to the development of healthy relations among ethnic groups. Many conflicts are sustained by stereotypes, myths or prejudices that remain active at household, neighbourhood or national levels. Such distortions may be based on feelings of superiority; on a belief that ethnic groups are "fundamentally" different and therefore cannot solve their differences through peaceful means; on the assumption that some groups are "inherently" aggressive and have a hidden imperialistic agenda; or that some groups are lazy, unreliable, parasitic or distrustful of outsiders. Stereotypes generate feelings of fear and hatred, which may entrench ethnic boundaries and weaken the reins of moderation when conflicts break out. Here the churches have a contribution to make: based on the richness of their tradition they can help deconstruct myths, stereotypes and prejudices that impede the appreciation and respect of others in their irreducible otherness (See §§161-168 on inter-religious dialogue).

3. The International level

86. Some issues cannot be addressed at a local or national level; the involvement of organisations at the international level is required. For the churches the reality of the church universal, the notion of catholicity, the existence of the World Council of Churches, and the presence of the Christian world communions provide structures in which such issues may need to be addressed.

87. In many situations the decisions taken by powerful foreign countries, and by international organizations such as the World Bank, the International Monetary Fund and the World Trade Organization, need to be opposed. Some critiques of these bodies contend that, through their policies and rules, they impose on individual governments a set of macro-economic measures which (according to the Trade and Development Reports of the United Nations Conference on Trade and Development) have led to greater inequality among and within nations, tending to weaken the poorer countries and sectors of society even further. Churches need to offer an informed and responsible critique of economic policies which increase inequality within and between nations. This too is part of the churches' work for healing and a just reconciliation.

V. Biblical Perspectives

A. Methods and commitments

88. In reading and understanding biblical texts, a wide range of different approaches may be used and brought to interact as Christians engage with each other in order to explore the meaning of the biblical witness. As insights are gained from biblical texts with regard to ethnic identity, national identity, and the search for the unity of the church, the diversity of approaches which Christians use come together in a common understanding of their mutual accountability. They understand themselves accountable:

1. to the text as part of scripture;
2. to the church and its life; and
3. to the contexts in which both biblical exegetes and the local churches find themselves.

89. This sense of accountability leads to a number of commitments:

1. to treat the texts faithfully;

2. to address levels of meaning and the use - as well as the misuse - of biblical texts; and

3. to respect each others' individual contexts and different methods of interpretation, but also to challenge and support each other in fulfilling these responsibilities and commitments.

In this study, the local self-studies have helped to underline the crucial role of an ethically responsible reading of scripture.

90. Readers and interpreters may discipline their reading by using specific critical methods; but readings will also be informed by personal perspectives and by contextual location. Individual perspectives are critically questioned, as well as broadened and enriched, as dialogue is initiated. In such dialogue, cross-cultural comparisons uncover the ethnocentric perspectives of readers and interpreters in various contexts.

B. The use and misuse of biblical texts

91. The biblical texts illuminate the way in which identity is continually shaped and reshaped as individuals and groups interact with each other. Social scientists refer to this interactive process as one of an ongoing "negotiation" of identity. Identities continue to develop in response both to changes within the group, and to the changing cultural and historical contexts in which the group lives. Issues of power and dominance (as occur in many majority/minority relationships) often determine - and significantly limit - the options available as identities develop. Such issues often lie at the roots of conflict within and between groups, and underlie the need felt, consciously or unconsciously, by many groups to define and affirm their own identity at the expense of others.

92. It is not possible to encapsulate all the various biblical notions of ethnic or national identity. The Bible can speak of a nation/people/ethnic group or a stranger/outsider in many different

ways. The biblical texts show these different ways in which groups define themselves and set up boundaries in order to distinguish themselves from others, especially in situations where self-identity becomes a particularly burning issue.

93. The markers of such boundaries may be religious, geographic, social, and cultural. The self-definition of a group is not stable, and shifts can regularly occur. Blood-ties and genealogies, even language, are used as identity markers by Ezra and Nehemiah in their laws prohibiting mixed marriages (Ezra 9-10; Neh. 13:23-30). In contrast, some New Testament writings, such as the letters of Paul and the Johannine literature, establish a distinction between physical and spiritual descent (Jn 1:13; 3:5-5; Gal 3:25-29; 4:29; Rom 8:12-17). Shifts like this between the Old and the New Testament raise the critical question whether Christianity, in its appropriation of Jewish traditions, has labelled Judaism as "the other", the one over against whom one marks a privileged self-understanding.

94. One should be constantly aware of the power of language and symbols, in the biblical material as well as in contemporary situations of conflict. The misuse of religion - including the misuse of religious language, scriptures, and rituals - to legitimise the assertion of identities at the expense of others, is only too evident. The way in which both groups and issues are stereotyped, or "tagged", is a significant feature of such processes, and biblical examples are sometimes uncritically cited in support. However, the question has also been raised to what extent the universalistic perspective of other biblical texts may be used, in certain contexts, to subdue the voice of minority groups. Misuse may happen through a selective practice of "proof-texting", and by taking biblical passages out of context.

95. Even more difficult is the possibility that the most "obvious" reading of a text can invite misuse. How do we deal with biblical narratives in which brutal conquest is presented as the fulfilment of divine promise, and thus may be used to justify policies of ethnic cleansing (Josh 7; 1 Sam 15; 1 Kings 18, 20)? The problem in these narratives is

an understanding of election, meaning that God favours one group over the other, "my people" over "other peoples": Israel may possess the privileged space which God has in mind for them, whereas other peoples are dispossessed. In Deuteronomy 7:1-6, the same self-assertion expresses itself as xenophobia. However, such "difficult" texts can be interpreted through an "internal" critique, by reading them in light of other biblical passages that present a corrective view through their visions of peaceful coexistence, hospitality and the inclusion of strangers. This means that Deuteronomy 7:1-6 cannot be read in isolation from the corrective that comes from Deuteronomy 10:17-19.

C. The impartiality of God

96. Deuteronomy 10:17-19 also conveys a strong conviction of divine election: the people of Israel are the chosen ones "out of all the peoples". This is the basis on which the classification in the passage is built. A clear distinction is made between the inhabitants and the aliens, between those who belong and those who do not, between the insiders and the outsiders — between those who are chosen and those who are not. This is the arrogance of the passage and, as the hermeneutics of otherness and alienation show, it may easily become authoritarian and destructive - despite its claim to charity.

97. However, in this passage from Deuteronomy a dynamic is introduced which helps control the potential arrogance of the "chosen": the God by whom they have been chosen, does not necessarily take their side. Indeed the great, the mighty and the terrible God who is not partial and takes no bribe, does not side with the strong but with the weak, executing justice for the fatherless and the widow, loving the sojourners and giving them food and clothing. The impartiality of God has, as its primary expression, a partial option for the weak and vulnerable. Arrogance and domination - be it violent or benevolent - cannot turn God to account. God's partial option for the poor and marginalised is an expression of God's mightiness, not in the remarkable Pauline version that the power of God becomes manifest in human weakness (2 Cor 4:5-11), but by relativising human power

structures rather than legitimating them. God as the Sovereign dismisses all human claims to superiority. The earth belongs to God who does not judge at "face value".

98. The passage in Deuteronomy further reminds the chosen of their own experience in the past, when they themselves were the weak and oppressed: "for you were strangers in the land of Egypt" (Deut 10:19). Their own history encourages empathy and the recognition of themselves in the other. Memory is mobilised as a means to make the crossing of barriers possible, yes, even the demolition of them. At one time or another we have all been strangers, the label of "otherness" could just as well be attached to ourselves.

99. In antiquity it was common that the human person established identity by demarcations of contrasts. Self-affirmation was gained by a repetitive pattern of exclusions. In the New Testament this pattern was converted from establishing *ex*clusivity to an expression of *in*clusivity. The best example is Galatians 3:26-28, where Paul probably cites a baptismal formula when he envisions that among those who have been baptised into Christ divisions based on ethnicity, social standing and gender no longer apply – they have all become one in Christ Jesus.

100. In the New Testament, the understanding of God as one who does not judge at "face value" is evident in gospel narratives about the ministry of Jesus as he extends God's love and mercy to the poor and the marginalised. This understanding serves to defend the crossing of a variety of boundaries (Acts 10:34; Rom 2:11; Eph 6:9; Col 3:25 and Jas 2:1). This crossing represents a violation of well-established standards, especially as the division between Jews and non-Jews is overcome. The social, cultural and religious underpinning of naming the "insiders" and the "outsiders" no longer follows established patterns, and those who had been marginalised become witnesses to the acts of God. Yes, those who were far off, aliens from the commonwealth of Israel, and strangers to the covenants of promise "have been brought near by the blood of Christ. For he is our peace; in his flesh he has

made both groups into one and has broken down the dividing wall, that is, the hostility between us." (Eph 2:13-14; see 2:11-22).

101. The parable of the Good Samaritan (Lk 10:25-37) is not limited to the encouragement of good deeds towards those in need even if they are considered enemies - however hard that lesson may be. Jesus' final question "Which of these three, do you think, was a neighbour to the man who fell into the hands of the robbers?" (10:36) invites the lawyer to take the perspective of the victim, to imagine how it feels to be on the receiving end. It relocates him from being the acting subject, the well-meaning giver of love. In order to remain a giver, he has to allow for the impossible to become possible: it takes him, as a Jew, to the point where his initial question can only be answered if he identifies with a Samaritan – one with whom he should share nothing (cf. Jn 4:9). This story of Jesus therefore attacks the established order by which groups and the relationship between them are defined in terms that fuel alienation and hostility. It does this by claiming that in the hands of the supposed "enemy", the impure other, mercy and care may be found.

D. Diversity in unity

102. Unity in its true and positive sense involves the creation of a new reality from components previously separated from one another. The biblical witness is that genuine unity bears diversity within it; unity is both "we" and the "other" brought into a new reality which includes both. For a genuine unity is not just the sum of its component parts, but reflects also their creative interaction within the whole. Indeed in a sense, meaning and creativity is the product of differences brought together within the larger whole.

103. Therefore, a genuine unity is not realised simply by the absorption of minorities into an already existing group. There are many examples of false "unities" which do not respect their own internal diversities, or achieve justice and reconciliation among their constituent parts. Strategies of inclusion which create "unity" at the

expense of the identities of the minority or the "other", are often an expression of dominance within the relationship. Such strategies often sow the seeds of future conflict and exclusion, both within a group and between groups. Realisations of unity must therefore respect the diversities which are being brought together into one new reality.

104. Genesis 10 presents the variety of peoples originating from one ancestor, Noah. In so doing, it signifies an understanding of human society as a collective entity which, while historically and politically distinct, yet is one family. Isaiah (Is 2:2; 11:10; 49:6; 60:3) envisioned the "nations" as included in God's salvation.

105. In their efforts to incorporate both Jews and Gentiles, the early Christian communities would employ corporate images such as that of flock and people (Jn 10:16; 11:52). They did so in ways that refused to recognize privilege based on ethnic descent. Thus it is not a case of Gentiles being incorporated into the Jewish people of God, but rather the formation of a single new people irrespective of their ethnic origin. This vision in the Gospel of John of a heterogeneous and multi-ethnic, yet inclusive community is rooted in the proclamations and promises made by Jesus.

106. Furthermore, because the emphasis is upon Jesus as the unifying centre, diverse ethnic groups are incorporated into a unified identity. They are brought into a relationship with each other through their common relationship to Jesus; and the believers are no longer defined, or define themselves, by their ethnic background, but rather by their faith in Jesus (Jn 3:15-16; 6:37, 40). The universal tenor of the message flows from the universal significance attached to Jesus himself. Because he is the light of the world (Jn 7:35; 10:16; 11:52; 12:20-22) he is not limited to any one nation, territory or time-period (Jn 7:35; 10:16; 11:52; 12:20-22). Other New Testament texts also witness to the fact that ethnic identities are not to be perceived as barriers dividing the one people of God (Lk 13:29; Acts 2:3-11; cf. also Rev 5:9; 21:24, 26).

107. But does this vision of an "inclusive" community actually represent a universalising strategy which actually aims to eradicate differences rather than to include and value them? Is the vision not multi-ethnic but *trans*-ethnic in its outlook and perspective - entailing the danger that one ethnic group or culture becomes (or continues to be) the dominant voice, while pretending to be non-specific and non-dominant? This danger must be borne in mind, and countered. Only when the equal value of different ethnic identities within the community of believers is asserted in ways that reject the manipulation of ethnic tagging in order to keep "the other" in a subordinate and despised place, can the biblical vision of a truly *multi*-ethnic community come closer to fruition.

E. A ministry of reconciliation

108. As stressed in §§102-107, a genuine unity is based on just relations among its component parts. Whatever reconciliation is necessary among these parts must be achieved in order for the unity to be genuine, and lasting. A paradigm of reconciliation between individuals, ethnic groups or nations can be found in the reconciliation between Jacob (Israel) and Esau (Edom) in Genesis 32-33. The conflict between the twin brothers configures also ethnic tension and rivalry over territory. In order to return home, Jacob must face the problem of his broken relationship with Esau. He shows repentance and good faith as he appeases his brother through gifts which are more than generous. Reconciliation is achieved because there has been a re-establishment of justice, through Jacob's return of the blessing which he had stolen from Esau. To be sure, Jacob could not fully compensate Esau for what he had lost, but was ready in his heart to make an honest "return" so as to restore justice. The witness of this biblical story - whether it reflects a peace historically made between Judah and Edom, or a hope that twin brothers like Esau and Jacob can reach reconciliation after a story of strife - suggests that reconciliation is possible if there is a conversion of heart and a genuine attempt to engage the issue of justice. Reconciliation requires

that the contending parties take the initiative to face what is required in order that restitution can be made

109. According to 2 Corinthians 5:17-21 those who are in Christ are a new creation from God, made possible because God, in Christ, has reconciled the world to himself. This divine reconciliation is further expressed in a ministry of reconciliation, whereby God has entrusted the message of reconciliation to Christians as ambassadors of Christ. Their service as ministers of reconciliation is intrinsically bound to God's act of reconciliation and righteousness, a gracious gift freely given, with no distinctions attached – since God is one (Rom 3:21-30).

110. This paradigm of reconciliation entails also a kenotic dimension. The recognition of the power of the powerless in relation to the love of God is at the centre of the one of the earliest Christians hymns, which Paul quotes in Philippians 2:5-11. The pre-eminent example is Christ Jesus

> who, though he was in the form of God, did not regard equality with God as something to be exploited, but emptied himself, taking the form of a slave, being born in human likeness. And being found in human form, he humbled himself and became obedient to the point of death - even death on a cross.

Christians should be Christ-like, doing nothing from selfish ambition or conceit, but in humility regarding others as better than themselves (cf. Phil 2:3, cf. also Mk 8:35/Lk 9:23). Paradoxically, weakness may in fact be the utmost strength, and at the last supper Jesus instructs his disciples that greatness is to be "as one who serves" (Lk 22:27; see 22:24-27).

VI. Theological Perceptions

111. The starting point for a Christian response to ethnic and nation-

al conflict has been the challenge of the identity Christians receive
and share in baptism (see §§1, 5, 40 and 99 above), and the implications this has for the life and mission of the church. In the Nicene
creed we confess "one baptism for the forgiveness of sins", and this
one baptism is a sacramental bond of unity. This perspective has been
paramount throughout this study document, and it will be further
explored in what follows.

112. From this uniting baptismal theology there emerges a call for reconciliation, for overcoming sin and alienation, for providing healing.
As an agent in God's mission of reconciliation the church should be
a living witness to the unity which we confess, and be an effective and
prophetic sign of the fullness of communion with God into which
the whole of creation will be gathered.

113. In the following we first reflect on how baptism and eucharist are
constitutive in granting the divine gift of unity and reconciliation to
which the churches are called to bear witness. We then move to
explore how a process towards reconciliation must include reflection
upon truth-telling, justice and the exercise of power, culminating in
the reconciliation of memories.

A. Baptism and eucharist

1. Baptism

a. Prophetic sign

114. Baptism is a sign of the *basileia* of God, and of the life of
renewed communities. In a situation where churches are divided, the
affirmation of *Baptism, Eucharist and Ministry* is vital: "Our common
baptism, which unites us to faith in Christ, is thus a basic bond of
unity. We are one people and are called to confess and serve one Lord
in each place and in all the world."[13] The gift of unity in baptism is,

---

[13] *Baptism, Eucharist and Ministry*, Faith & Order Paper No. 111, Geneva, World
Council of Churches, 1982, "Baptism", §6, p. 3.

among other things, a prophetic sign to local communities divided by ethnic and religious violence, providing insights and trajectories for the exercise, by the churches, of the ministry of reconciliation.

115. There are, of course, still divisions which impair the churches' unity and hamper their common witness and service. As *Unitatis Redintegratio* says: "Baptism establishes a sacramental bond of unity among all who through it are reborn",[14] it goes on to acknowledge the fact that, despite this claim, our "unity" is not yet visible unity amongst the churches. The gift of unity in baptism is therefore a challenge to the churches to recognize their accountability to one another, to overcome their divisions, and to manifest visibly their fellowship. Baptism into union with Christ calls churches to be open and honest with one another, bestowing upon them both the freedom and the responsibility to journey toward common proclamation of the Word, confession of the one faith, celebration of one eucharist, and full sharing in one ministry. The more their unity is manifest, and the more their fellowship flourishes, the more effective the churches' common witness to just reconciliation and healing will be.

b. Personal identity and the new community in Christ

116. In baptism men and women, individuals, die to established loyalties and are born into a new relationship, a new community whose allegiance is to Christ. God has called women and men out of ethnic groups, nations, languages and races, and incorporated them into God's new people by baptism. In being baptised by water there is a new beginning, one which removes the effects of personal and corporate sin. In being baptised by water we are made one with God as God's children, members of the body of Christ and inheritors of the *basileia* of God.

117. In this new community, a community able to celebrate diversity, a man or woman can no longer expect to think or speak in terms of

---

[14] *Vatican II - Constitutions, Decrees and Declarations*, ed. A. Flannery, O.P., New York, Costello Publishing Company, 1996, §22, p.520.

"I", but rather "we". As Christians mature, their faith grows into deeper participation in the faith confessed, celebrated and witnessed to by the "we" of the Christian community, both locally and world-wide, both now and through the ages. Within the new community in Christ, the "I believe" of personal commitment, in its integrity and uniqueness, discovers its home within the "we believe" of the Christian community as a whole.

118. In a situation of ethnic conflict, the new community in Christ is called to embody, and witness to, just reconciliation and healing. Because the "we" has been transformed and reordered – men and women have been called out of particular ethnic and national loyalties and made one in Christ – then the new community may be an effective sign of God's will for humanity. The experiences of this new community can inform the analysis of areas of conflict, and point to positive actions by the community to reduce tension and conflict, and to foster justice and reconciliation.

2. The eucharist

119. The gifts given by God through the Holy Spirit in baptism are renewed every time the eucharist is celebrated. Baptismal faith is re-affirmed and grace given for the faithful living out of the Christian calling. In this celebration the members of the church are judged, transformed, reordered, and nourished. It is in the receiving of the body and blood of Christ that we are incorporated into Christ and empowered for mission.

120. Just as baptism is inseparable from a life of service and witness, so too the Lord's supper demands reconciliation and sharing among all those regarded as brothers and sisters in the one family of God.[15] Because the Lord's supper is the sacrament which builds up community, all kinds of injustice, racism, estrangement, and lack of freedom are radically challenged when we share in the body and blood of Christ. God's judgement demands that our behaviour be consistent

---

[15] *Baptism, Eucharist and Ministry*, "Eucharist", §20, p. 14.

with the reconciling presence of God in human history. Thus the eucharist requires – and empowers - the churches' witness for justice and reconciliation in situations of injustice and conflict.

121. Moreover, in the celebration of the eucharist the church witnesses to, and is a sign of, the *basileia* of God. The Melbourne World Mission Conference (1980) envisioned the very structure of the eucharist as a radical witness for justice and unity both within and outside the church itself, characterising the liturgical parts of the service in this way:

- The welcome - irrespective of race, class, caste or gender;

- The forgiveness - in ethnic conflicts, forgiveness makes the community accountable for its past and is freed from it for a reconciled future;

- The peace - being right with God, each other and the creation;

- The sharing - the right and equal use of resources.[16]

122. Furthermore at the offertory, members of the congregation bring themselves and the world to be offered to God, an offering which is returned and renewed providing a fresh impetus for life. In the equal sharing in the sacramental elements, the unequal sharing of the world's resources is judged: *here* is an effective sign in the midst of ethnic and national conflict!

B. The ministry of reconciliation and healing

123. God's mission is to reconcile human community, establishing a situation in which differences are promoted and celebrated, and where

---

[16] Cf. *Your Kingdom Come: Mission Perspectives, Report on the World Conference on Mission and Evangelism, Melbourne, Australia, 12 - 25 May 1980*, Geneva, Commission on World Mission and Evangelism, World Council of Churches, 1980, pp. 205-206.

human beings live in harmony with nature, with each other and with God. This is sometimes expressed in the idea of the *basileia* of God, which already is, but has yet to come to fulfilment. By its nature and its mission, the church as the people of God is called to participate and share in God's mission. It is a community which, in worship, is fed, encouraged, and sent out. It is sent out both to witness to, and to exercise, empowering and vulnerable love both within and beyond the boundaries of the church. The church is invited to work with non-Christian brothers and sisters because (as recognized by some) God's will to save encompasses all.

124. As noted in §104, Genesis 10 attempts to mirror human society as such, as it is at any time in its history. The nations are conceived as politically and historically distinct from one another, but they originate from one ancestor, Noah. Such a profound consciousness of the unity of humankind offers an "unparalleled ecumenical vision of human reality."[17] However, because of human hubris God scatters the nations across the face of the earth. The task of the chosen people, as a light to the nations, is to re-establish the primordial unity given to them as a gift from God their creator. Such a task is at the heart of the ministry of reconciliation. The primary identity marker is the common humanity of the nations, a common identity in which their differences are not dissolved.

125. The church is called to hold together the invitation to be both an effective and a prophetic sign. It is to be an effective sign by the way in which different cultures, in their diversity, live and work together within it. It is a prophetic sign when, in situations of ethnic and national conflict, it denounces injustice and discrimination, actively working to remove them by seeking means of reconciliation.

126. The church is called to take God as its source and model of administering justice. God's justice, especially in the Old Testament, is often presented in terms of a cosmic harmony, a state in which

---

[17] Walter Brueggemann, *Genesis*, Interpretation Bible Commentary, Atlanta, John Knox Press, 1982, p.94.

human beings and all creatures live together in harmony with each other and with the whole of the natural order. This is the type of justice and reconciliation that the church is invited to exercise, by being "stewards" of creation and co-creators with God. This is a true stewardship involving neither domination nor exploitation, but rather the proper use of the world's material resources in order to satisfy responsibly the needs of present and future generations. Theologically, therefore, reconciliation emphasises the mission that God entrusts to the church: a mission in which Christians are called to be good stewards and to manage resources in a just and equitable manner.

127. When Christians affirm that they are created in God's image, they recognize that reconciliation can be understood neither as the negation of cultural and ethnic differences, nor as a reason for suppressing or dominating others on the basis of false claims to superiority. God's image is expressed by and in ethnic and national identities; it is an image which is open to differences but which promotes justice and respect for the other. When they are employed positively and not negatively, cultures (including their languages, traditions and symbols) are *loci* where God reveals God's self to human beings.

128. The church however, cannot be an effective and prophetic sign if it does not live out its nature and mission. The churches recognize, with humility, that sometimes Christians have used violence, based upon their reading and interpretation of the scriptures (cf. the biblical reflections in §§91-95). Sometimes theology has been used to justify discrimination: the system of apartheid, for instance, was based on a theological error, namely the view that white people are superior to black people. The churches recognize that they have been agents of violence and discrimination. Announcing the Good News, especially in "mission" countries, has often been marked by ethnocentric racist practices and ideologies. The churches are called to recognize, with humility, the fact that - knowingly or unknowingly - violence has been committed in the name of God.

129. In such situations, Christians forget the strength that lies in the

power of the cross of Christ. Rather they are tempted to use power, forgetting that, in giving himself, Jesus has been able to save us through an act of self-effacement which has become a source of strength and salvation. Christians are often afraid to lose themselves, and yet it is in losing one's life for Christ's sake that one will find it (cf. Mt 10:39, Mt 16:25). Here is the paradox: that weakness can in reality be strength, as the biblical witness also has shown (see §110).

130. Both history and the world today place before us cases of ethnic, national, and other forms of violence, which have been used to demean and objectify the other. Extreme right wing movements, nationalistic political parties, xenophobia, genocide, ethnic cleansing and racism – all are usually grounded in an ethnocentrism which denies the other the right to exist in his or her difference. These situations challenge Christians to renew themselves in their mission as agents of reconciliation, as healers of the wounds and hurts of human beings. Christians are invited to transform situations of conflict and violence, because whatever dehumanises human beings distorts God's image in everyone.

131. More specifically, in situations of ethnic violence or the denial of legitimate differences Christians can find inspiration in the scriptures, where the people of God, and God's *basileia*, are comprised of people of different races and languages coming from the different corners of the world. The biblical reflections in §§102-107 have highlighted the fact that the biblical understanding of unity does not exclude difference. Ethnic differences, therefore, should never be used as grounds for justifying discrimination, injustice or violence.

132. Even though violence and conflict are pervasive, the churches must guard against a pessimism leading to the belief that human beings are to be mistrusted, and incapable of surmounting the problems of conflict and violence. Violence is *not* inevitable. If it is indeed a social construct, then it is a result of what human beings have decided to do, or not to do. But in co-operation with the grace of God, especially mediated through the Holy Spirit, Christians are empow-

ered to eliminate that which disfigures humankind.

133. To summarise: for reconciliation and healing to be accomplished, the root causes of ethnic violence need to be uncovered. As noted, to undertake this adequately theology will need to appropriate tools from the social sciences. For example, ethnic and national conflicts are often linked to schemes to seize, exploit, and even take away resources that rightfully belong to others. But the equitable use and sharing of created goods can never mean depriving their rightful owners of resources which are their basic means of livelihood. As stewards, the churches are called to participate in evolving a just economic system, one that neither creates imbalances in human and state relations, nor disturbs ecosystems.

134. Christians have a unique calling to participate in God's ministry of reconciliation; yet it is imperative that they co-operate with, and learn from, people of other faiths, beliefs and convictions. God identifies with all that God has created. Christ died for the whole of humankind. His salvific mission, as carried out in his lifetime and especially on the cross, extends to all human beings. And Christians believe that each human being has something to contribute towards God's mission to reconcile the world, as that mission was realised in Christ and continued through the Holy Spirit.

1. The process of reconciliation

135. Healing and transforming situations of conflict and tension requires the churches to be clear about the process of reconciliation. Faced with the urgency of their ministry of reconciliation, the churches risk not preparing themselves properly to initiate it. Where there is mistrust and past hurts, healing and reconciliation cannot be achieved quickly.

136. Victims and victimisers can be individuals or communities. In concrete human situations, it is sometimes difficult to determine who is the victim and who is the offender (victimiser): there are occasions

when the offenders portray themselves as victims; and there are victims who suddenly turn, becoming offenders whilst maintaining the role of a victim. However, for the sake of clarity, we will presume [situations in which] there is a clear distinction between the two.

137. The constitutive elements in the process of reconciliation should be: confession and truth-telling, a request for forgiveness, and the requirements of justice. These need not occur in any set order; in some cases, for example, forgiveness comes before confession.

a. Truth-telling, confession and forgiveness

138. A process of reconciliation will normally start by the offender taking the first step to tell the truth about what happened, hoping that the victim will accept this gesture. It is not enough to say what happened; confession should normally be accompanied by a request for pardon. This can take different forms, including public confession or more discreet means. What is important is to ensure that whatever channels are used, there should be sincerity and openness.

139. In some cases the victim refuses to participate in the search for reconciliation and healing. Patience is required in order to find a more opportune moment to re-launch the process. Attempts should be made to discover how confession and truth telling is undertaken in different cultural settings. In some cases, it may involve the use of rituals which employ symbols. Sometimes opportunities to effect reconciliation have been missed because the wrong means have been employed or, worse, imposed.

b. The requirements of justice

140. Forgiveness is not given automatically; it comes when the victim responds to the request for pardon. Many people are willing to forgive, but the requirements of justice should never be forgotten - even if the victim does not ask for them. In South Africa, credit must be given to the Truth and Reconciliation Commission (TRC) for the

work it did in reconciliation and in healing the wounds caused by the system of apartheid. Notwithstanding this, the TRC has been criticised for providing neither the room nor the conditions in which justice is both done, and seen to be done. Some have suggested that the Commission should have addressed the issues of compensation, restoration and restitution. Some public and political apologies (for instance that of Germany for its massacre of the Herero in Namibia between 1904 and 1907, and of Belgium's complicity in the murder of Patrice Lumumba)have been weakened by the demand that claims for reparations will not be made. Promises by these countries to give aid to their former colonies underrate the importance of justice in the process of reconciliation.

141. It is to be hoped that at the end of the process of reconciliation there will be a healing of past hurts, and the construction of a new community. This will depend largely on how the different "stake holders" have participated in the whole process. The government, civil society organizations, Christians, members of other religions and even international organizations, all have a role to play, because reconstruction and reconciliation often require putting in place services and infrastructures which call for the participation of more than one stake holder. The resettling of refugees, for example, calls not only for the rebuilding of the infrastructure, but also the involvement of the United Nations High Commission for Refugees (UNHCR) to settle disputes resulting from illegal occupation of land belonging to those forced to leave their territory. Reconstruction of a new community takes a long time, because healing human hurts requires that the necessary conditions for rebuilding confidence have been put in place.

142. Even when all has been done to bring the process successfully to this point, it should never be imagined that reconciliation and healing can start and end at a given moment in time. Psycho-social trauma caused by acts of violence, including rape or the mistreating of vulnerable groups such as children and the elderly, require time to heal and are difficult to address within a given time framework. Christian communities have a unique role to play in addressing such hurts,

which require a more personal and discreet approach.

c. Justice and power

143. Political power derives its legitimacy from the goal of just relationships. Justice is the norm for creative living in society, irrespective of the particular social and political order. The tendency for hierarchies is to accumulate and concentrate power in its different forms; the biblical witness critically reflects the concern for the limitation and redistribution of power - that is, a downward distribution and sharing of power. The relationship between justice for, and love of, one's neighbour corrects the pattern of accumulation and unjust distribution of power.

144. The theological criteria for God's option for the poor hint at the need for the empowerment of the powerless, and a preference for the victims of oppression and exclusion. It was the task of Israel's king to sit in the gate of the city hearing the orphan, the widow and the stranger voice their needs, and to act on their behalf.[18] Here is a model for the church in its prophetic witness against the unjust use of power, and in its participation in God's life-giving empowerment of the marginalised and redistribution of resources for the benefit of all.

145. The churches can act in a credible manner only if they have addressed, and repented of, their own historic - and contemporary - support for and use of national and imperial power. This applies in the past particularly to the crusades and to the churches participation in the slave trade and colonial conquest; and, in the present, to their collusion in the exercise of unjust economic, political and military power.

146. Power and leadership are intimately related. If the church is to be an effective sign, then the manner in which leadership is exercised is itself part of God's mission. While it is true that leadership is exer-

---

[18] See 2 Samuel 15 - the means by which Absalom usurps the throne.

cised differently in different contexts and situations there is, nonethe-less, a particular Christian insight in this area (see again the discussion in §110). Jesus did not use the language of service to disempower peo-ple. Jesus did not abdicate his role as leader but exercised that leader-ship in such a way that the needs of others were met, in order that they could become free, responsible human beings, human beings enabled to take responsibility for themselves and others in the community.

2. The reconciliation of memories

147. Human development, and all acquired knowledge, are to a great extent based on the ability to organize and take advantage of memo-ry. Without memory human beings cannot take advantage of what they have learned or experienced. Memory enables what once was heard, read, observed or experienced, and what has been practised, to be brought into the present. Memory enables every human being to function effectively.

148. In a religious context Christians are accustomed, both as individ-uals and as congregations, to employ memory in the eucharist as the bread is broken and the wine outpoured "in remembrance of" Him. Technically this is referred to as the *anamnesis*. Through it, the celebrat-ing community not only brings the past into the present - "remem-bers" - but appropriates the effects of what God has done in the life, death and resurrection of Jesus of Nazareth. When a congregation celebrates the eucharist, through the recalling of what Christ has done the church is both challenged and empowered to be an effective sign of God's mission.

149. Secular communities also remember. The exercise of community memory - the collective memory of particular communities - brings their stories of past events into the present. This memory tends to preserve their story of the past, encouraging continuity rather than change. It does the work of tradition. Community memory, like *anam-nesis*, needs places and events where commemorations can take place.

150. Yet community memory, even if it exists in a written, fixed form, is not necessarily uniform and dominant. It may harbour a subversive potential. The past – as a source of self-understanding and value – is not a "neutral zone", but an arena in which the status and identity of groups are contested. These efforts to control the meaning of the past are frequently embodied in a struggle for the possession and "correct" interpretation of the community memory. (On these issues see also §77).

151. The process of reconciling memories within communities in which conflict has been evident can be undertaken in a number of different ways. There follow examples of this process from Ireland, Switzerland and South Africa, each with its own particular focus.

152. The local self-study on Ireland showed how the role of community memory has a vital place in maintaining and continuing, over a period of three hundred years, ethnic-religious conflict. The past is brought into the present by commemorations of past events, in which for example marches of representative groups from both sides of the conflict witness to, and commemorate, their own community memories. The events of the past cannot be re-enacted; but historical events persist in the community memory, events which can be revisited and renegotiated. As noted, in community memory history can be conveniently forgotten, or recovered to suit the community's perceived ideological or other needs.

153. The people of Ireland, taken as a whole, have participated in shared events; but the divided communities have no *common* history of what has taken place, and no community memory. Their different memories of the past hold each community imprisoned, so that peacemaking and reconciliation is impeded. The Irish School of Ecumenics initiated a process entitled the "Reconciliation of Memories".[19] In small communities along the border between North and South, people met together to retell their stories of shared events

---

[19] *Reconciling Memories*, ed. Alan D. Falconer and Joseph Liechty, Dublin, The Columba Press, 1998.

and to negotiate a common history, a common memory as a step towards reconciliation. Memories of the past have to be redeemed, so that the pain and the hurts can be healed. Only then can peacemaking be fully pursued.

154. In Switzerland theologians from different denominations have undertaken the reappraisal of church history by writing that history together,[20] and thereby facing and renegotiating even their most controversial and identity-shaping events. This is not an easy therapy. Such a reconciliation of memories involves an acceptance of responsibility for the hurt in the memory of the other. *Then* the potential for cleansing memories is possible.

155. The Truth Commission in South Africa had, as its rationale and working principle, the conviction that publicly articulated memory may provide a discourse of justice for the victims and remorse for the perpetrators, enabling them to move forward together in restoring social and political order. Through a painful appropriation and recognition of common vulnerability, each empowers the other to be free. Only then will the vicious circle, in which the victim so easily becomes perpetrator, be broken.

C. Christian unity and inter-confessional dialogue

156. The Canberra Unity Statement (1991)[21] has as its title, "The Unity of the Church as Koinonia: Gift and Calling". The Statement has many declarations pertinent to the subject matter of this study document; among these are:

- The purpose of the church is to unite people with Christ in the power of the Spirit, to manifest communion in prayer and action and to point to the fullness of

---

[20] *Ökumenische Kirchengeschichte der Schweiz.* hg. v. Lukas Vischer / Lukas Schenker / Rudolf Dellsperger, Freiburg Schweiz/Basel 1994, 2. Aufl. 1998.

[21] *The Ecumenical Movement: An Anthology of Key Texts and Voices,* ed. Michael Kinnamon and Brian E. Cope, Geneva, WCC Publications and Grand Rapids, Michigan, Wm. B. Eerdmans Publishing Co, 1997, pp.124-125.

communion with God, humanity and the whole of creation in the glory of the kingdom.

- The calling of the church is to proclaim reconciliation and provide healing, to overcome divisions based on race, gender, age, culture, and to bring people into communion with God.

157. Further, the text reflects on how their disunity is detrimental to the churches' ability to participate effectively in the mission of God. The language of Christian unity has been developed by the Canberra Statement, in that unity is perceived as a gift which God has already given, whilst the calling of the churches is to make that unity visible.

158. Prior to the Canberra assembly, Faith and Order published *Church & World*.[22] This noted that the churches have tended to separate their common concern for, and service of, the world from their efforts to make visible that unity of the church which is its common gift and calling. The challenge to the churches was to hold these two aspects together - as indicated in the subtitle of the document, "The Unity of the Church and the Renewal of Human Community".[23]

159. It is understandable that when churches are faced with ethnic and national conflicts and the resultant human suffering, there is a desire to deal with the situation immediately. The often slow progress of inter-confessional dialogue is gently pushed to one side and by-passed. Yet the effectiveness of the churches' ministry of reconciliation is undermined when the cause of making God's gift of unity visible is ignored.

160. Thus inter-confessional dialogue is an essential part of the

---

[22] *Church and World: The Unity of the Church and the Renewal of Human Community*, Faith and Order Paper No. 151, 2nd, revised printing, Geneva, WCC Publications, 1990.
[23] On this see most recently Melanie A. May, "The Unity We Share, the Unity We Seek", in *A History of the Ecumenical Movement: Volume 3, 1968-2000*, ed. John Briggs, Mercy Amba Oduyoye and Georges Tsetsis, Geneva, WCC Publications, 2004, pp. 83-102, esp. p. 89, 97.

churches' response to situations in which there is ethnic and national conflict. In many places this dialogue has already commenced, but will require a fresh impetus. In other situations there will have been significant agreements which need to be harvested. For some situations, the dialogue will need to begin. Faith & Order has produced over many years a series of instruments which have been designed to help churches in their inter-confessional dialogues - *Baptism, Eucharist & Ministry* and *The Nature and Purpose of the Church*[24], to name but two. Whatever the situation, structures to enable the leadership of the churches to maintain contact will be an urgent priority, both at local and national levels.

D. Inter-religious dialogue

161. The local self-studies have shown that religion can play an important role in precipitating violence: in the Sudan it is Islam; in India, Hinduism; in Sri Lanka, Buddhism; and in Fiji, Christianity. What initiatives can local churches take in such situations?

162. Where reconciliation involving religious communities is sought, mutual understanding and truth telling is the first step in a process of peace-making and the creation of a renewed community in which there is justice and mutual care. Such a process is called "inter-religious dialogue". To participate in this involves asking the question, "Is God's saving presence to be found in the religious life of our non-Christian neighbours?"[25] The World Mission Conference in San Antonio (1989) summed up the position with the following affirmation:

---

[24] *The Nature and Purpose of the Church: A Stage on the Way to a Common Statement*, Faith and Order Paper no. 181, Geneva, WCC/Faith and Order, November, 1998. As of 2005 the current version of this study document is *The Nature and Mission of the Church - A stage on the way to a common statement*, Faith and Order Paper No. 198.
[25] Many Christians still feel that participating in inter-religious dialogue is a betrayal of their allegiance to Christ. The biblical witness to be found in John 14:6 and Acts 4:12 is, for many, determinative in their turning aside from dialogue with their non-Christian neighbours.

> We cannot point to any other way of salvation than Jesus
> Christ; at the same time we cannot set limits to the sav-
> ing power of God.[26]

163. An attempt to go beyond the San Antonio affirmation was
undertaken by the WCC at a consultation on Theology of Religions
at Baar, Switzerland (1990). The consultation stated:

> This conviction that God as creator of all is present and
> active in the plurality of religions makes it inconceivable
> to us that God's saving activity could be confined to any
> one continent, cultural type, or group of people. A
> refusal to take seriously the many and diverse testi-
> monies to be found among nations and peoples of the
> whole world amounts to disowning the biblical testimo-
> ny to God as creator of all things and Father of
> humankind.[27]

164. It is thus possible, in good conscience, to participate in inter-religious dialogue without betraying one's allegiance to Christ. Rather, in
seeking reconciliation in situations of religious conflict Christians
truly participate in the mission of God, which is the reconciliation of
all human beings to each other and to God.

165. In many situations the churches may pursue their ministry of reconciliation through initiating or supporting inter-religious dialogue.
As noted above, there is a strong tradition of ecumenical reflection on
inter-religious dialogue as well as guidelines for its conduct. Some
principles on which such guidelines can be based are suggested below.

---

[26] *The San Antonio Report, Your Will be Done: Mission in Christ's Way*, ed. Frederick R.
Wilson, Geneva, WCC Publications, 1990, Report of Section I, §26, p. 32. This is
cited in the most recent text addressing these issues: "Religious Plurality and
Christian Self-Understanding", Geneva, Inter-religious Relations, Mission and
Evangelism, and Faith and Order, §23.
[27] "Religious Plurality: Theological Perspectives and Affirmations", Geneva, WCC
Sub-unit on Dialogue with People of Living Faiths and Ideologies, 1990, p. 2. This
too is cited in the recent text "Religious Plurality and Christian Self-
Understanding", §24.

Guidelines for inter-religious dialogue: basic principles

166. The basis of inter-religious dialogue[28] must be a process of mutual empowerment, rather than a negotiation between parties who have conflicting interests and claims. Such dialogue:

1. *begins when people meet each other;*

Everyday contact with neighbours and sharing the similarities and differences in their lifestyles is possible because people share a common humanity, created in the image of God.

2. *depends upon the willingness to listen to one another;*

Real meetings take place when people listen carefully to what each has to say to the other and allowing each participant to describe their religious convictions in their own terms.

3. *makes it possible to share in service to the community;*

Human communities depend upon the contribution of all its parts if they are to be effective. Sharing in witness against all that diminishes human dignity and human community builds mutual trust. Such sharing is further enhanced as each part brings its own distinctive insights to social issues.

4. *becomes the medium of authentic witness.*

Where all participants are encouraged to share their deep-

---

[28] Cf. the 1979 Guidelines from the WCC: "Guidelines on Dialogue with People of Living Faiths and Ideologies", Geneva, World Council of Churches, 1979. For further advice on how to undertake inter-religious dialogue see *Ecumenical Considerations for Dialogue and Relations with People of Other Religions: Taking Stock of 30 years of dialogue and revisiting the 1979 guidelines*, Geneva, WCC Publications, 2003.

est religious convictions, all have the potential to discover new insights into the truths that are shared and rediscover truths that have been neglected.

Such a process can help the participants to recognize the image of God in the other.

167. Whilst inter-religious dialogue is an important process leading to mutual understanding and trust and, further, to common activity on behalf of the well being of the community, it is not an end in itself. If the process of reconciliation is to go on, it is important to create structures which will continue to build and maintain bridges between religious communities, structures that will stand the test of possible future strife. The creation of inter-religious councils[29] in which community leaders participate is, in most cases, an appropriate next step after inter-religious dialogue.

168. Inter-religious dialogue may lead the churches to a new awareness of difficulties or injustices suffered by their dialogue partner. In exercising their prophetic witness, the churches may need to request that nation states and other political entities protect minority religious communities. At the same time, the churches may need to encourage self-restraint on the part of the majority religious tradition. In every political structure it is vital that space is made for all religious traditions.

VII. Participating in God's Mission

169. The analysis of situations of conflict in this study document has been based upon the notion of identity, whether marked by ethnicity or nation, tribe or race. Such identity markers are powerful motivators in situations in which groups seek for power and resources at the expense of others. In baptism Christians are incorporated into Christ,

---

[29] See *Ethnicity, National Identity & Church Unity: A Study on Fiji 2001*, pp. 49-51.

and this identity marker takes precedence over all others, which may then be celebrated in their turn (see §§1, 5, 40, 99, 111, and 114-118 above). One of the great steps forward in the response of the churches to God's gift of unity has been a common recognition of each other's baptism. Such a sign of unity needs the witness of the local churches as a celebration of the sign of the unity of humankind.

170. The gifts which God gives Christians in baptism, are renewed and re-empowered every time the eucharist is celebrated (see §§115, 119-123, and 149 above). Whilst there is still much to be achieved, where eucharistic hospitality is now possible this sign of unity needs the witness of the local churches as a celebration of God's mission to reconcile all human beings to God's self. The eucharist is both a fore-taste of what is to come and a challenge to human beings to welcome each other, irrespective of ethnic, national, tribal or racial identities. The challenge in the light of God's forgiveness is to be freed from the past; this happens through acknowledging the errors of our ways and through the reconciliation of our memories and common history. The challenge in the light of receiving the consecrated elements of bread and wine is to share our finite resources equally with others.

171. The church is an effective and prophetic sign, a sign of God's *basileia*.[30] There is then a relationship between what the churches are, and their compelling involvement in the mission of God. As such the unity of the churches matters, for it has a direct relationship to their effective involvement in the mission of God. The local churches, in making visible the unity which God has given, are a sign of God's mission to create for God's self one new humanity, a sign to those entangled in ethnic and national conflicts. The local churches, in making their unity visible, are a prophetic sign that challenges and judges the manner in which conflicts have been created and continue. The local churches are an effective prophetic sign in order that situations of conflict may be ameliorated, healed and reconciled.

---

[30] See "Kingdom - Church - Humanity", chapter III in *Church & World*, pp 22-37.

172. The nature of the sign looks back to the ministry of Jesus of Nazareth in which the *basileia* of God drew near. In the actions and teaching of Jesus, boundaries are crossed and people are counted in, rather than excluded; the voice of forgiveness beyond what appears to be reasonable is heard; and justice is balanced in God's scales with equity. But above all, these words and actions are seen in terms of compassionate self-giving love. The body of Christ is summoned to replicate what Jesus said and did, and in that way to be an effective prophetic sign for the healing of conflicts within human communities.

173. Christians pray impatiently, every time the Lord's prayer is said, for the reign of God (*basileia*) to come. The nature of that *basileia* has been seen in the incarnation of the Word, and it looks forward to its completion in the future - for the church, whilst being a sign, is not that *basileia* but contains within itself hints, glimpses and imperfect representations of what will be. The images and visions of God's future are important to the churches, so that their involvement in the mission of God points in the right direction and travels on the right trajectories. These images and visions are conveyed by the scriptures, from which come also poetic, artistic and musical versions of the fulfilment of God's mission and the realisation of God's *basileia*.

174. The following lines of a hymn evoke such an image, one by which churches and Christians are challenged:[31]

> Already in the mind of God that city riseth fair:
> lo, how its splendour challenges the souls that greatly dare:
> yea, bids us seize the whole of life and build its glory there.

175. The "Invitation to the Churches" which follows summons them to act together as an effective prophetic sign in the context of ethnic and national conflicts. The invitation assumes that as they analyse the local situation carefully, and draw up an effective programme to be

---

[31] From the hymn "O Holy City, seen by John" by W. Russell Bowie (1882-1969), once of Grace Church, New York. The words of the hymn are based on Revelation 21.

followed, the churches will be acting ecumenically.

> May the God who raised Christ Jesus from the dead
> strengthen you to walk with him in his risen life, so that
> all, for whom Christ died may know God's peace with
> justice.

VIII. An Invitation to the Churches

176. This study has sought to describe how the churches, as an effective sign of the *basileia* of God, may participate in the mission of God
and in particular in the ministry of reconciliation. Material from the
study has been gathered together in this section in order to give local
churches a framework within which to analyse their situation and plan
a process of common reflection and action. As noted in §7 three
stages are suggested: analysis of the local situation, identifying sources
of conflict, and a process of common reflection and action.

177. As noted in §8, local congregations may want to begin their
analysis on their own but they should not proceed too far before join-
ing with congregations from other confessions, wherever that is possible.

A. Stage 1: Analysis of the local situation

178. Discuss the following questions, which (as noted in §§10 and 17)
have been considered by the local self-studies already conducted or
under way. You may find that not all of them apply to your own circumstances, or that some need to be adapted in order to be relevant.

1. What churches are present in your situation? What is
   their relationship to the various parties in tension or
   conflict? What is their relationship to each other, and to
   church or other bodies overseas?

2. How far do the divisions within – and among – the churches reflect divisions within society as a whole?

3. How do the churches understand, and address, issues of ethnic and national identity in your situation?

4. What do the churches understand to be their mission in your situation?

5. Upon what resources in Christian tradition do the churches draw in order to interpret- and offer hope within – your situation?

6. What external resources have the churches brought to bear on the situation?

7. How has the churches' engagement helped to effect change in your local situation?

8. What specific lessons have been learned about how the churches can help reduce tension and conflict, and promote a just peace, in your own context?

9. What have the churches learned from their engagement in this process about the unity of the church?

179. In responding to Question 3 ("How do the churches understand, and address, issues of ethnic and national identity in your situation?") you may find it helpful to consider the following questions, which have been gathered from section IV, "Perceptions from the Social Sciences" (§§40-87). Please remember that when using this material also you will need to contextualise it carefully; some aspects may not apply to your situation, or may need to be adapted.

Ethnicity

- Can you distinguish various ethnic groups in your

context?

- What characteristics define each as an ethnic group? (Physical characteristics, shared language, religion, etc. See §44)

Nationalism

- Can you distinguish national groups, as opposed to ethnic groups, in your context?
- What characteristics define each as a national group? (See §44)
- What political aspirations does each national group have?

Tribalism

- Can you distinguish various tribes in your context?
- What characteristics define the membership of these tribes?
- Does one tribe control the levers of power in this situation?

Racism

- Can you perceive racist attitudes within your context?
- Does one ethnic or national group perceive itself as superior to others?
- Is race a primary identity, embodying within itself ethnic and national identities?

Nation-state

- How did your nation-state come into being?
- In its foundation, did it inherit any factors which have lead to community conflict?
- Does your nation-state act in an equitable manner to all its peoples, or does it give certain groups preferential treatment?

Faith & State

- Has any faith tradition a close or exclusive association

with the state?
- Has any Christian tradition an exclusive association with the state?
- Does this association serve to legitimise the policies and actions of the state?
- Does this association both challenge and support the state in making equitable arrangements for all its citizens?

B. Stage 2: Identifying sources of conflict

180. Having analysed the situation in which your church finds itself, the next step is to understand why conflicts have arisen there. For this, the material under the following headings may be helpful. Again, each topic must be considered in light of your specific context; some topics may not apply, and others may need to be adapted. To help focus your discussion, you may wish for each topic to suggest questions analogous to those given in §181.

- Colonisation (§§68-69)

- Globalisation (§§70-71)

- Development (§§72-73)

- Power (§§74-78)

C. Stage 3: A programme of common reflection and action

181. Now is the time to draw up a positive programme by which you and your ecumenical partners can participate in God's mission, and in the ministry of reconciliation in particular. Here you may find the material in sections V on "Biblical Perspectives" (§§88-110) and VI on "Theological Perceptions" (§§111-166) helpful.

182. The following steps may offer the your churches a starting point for their common journey; you may need to adapt them, or adopt other projects, as appropriate for your own local situation. You are invited to:

- Renew your efforts to manifest the visible unity of the churches (cf. especially §§156-160)

- Ensure that your congregation(s) are aware of the priority of their baptismal identity (§§114-118), and its implications for the common life and witness of the churches

- Consider using the process of reconciliation discussed in §§135-142, bearing in mind also §§143-146

- Ask yourselves: Would the specific approach of the "Reconciliation of Memories" (§§147-155) be helpful in your own situation?

- Ask yourselves: Would it help in your own situation to initiate inter-religious dialogue (161-168), and subsequently to create inter-religious councils?

183. The Faith and Order Commission would welcome news of any study and action which you undertake locally, and would be grateful to receive any reports which result from your engagement with the issues of ethnic identity, national identity, and the search for the unity of the church. Material should be sent to: Faith and Order, World Council of Churches, 150, route de Ferney, 1211 Geneva 2, Switzerland.

Appendix

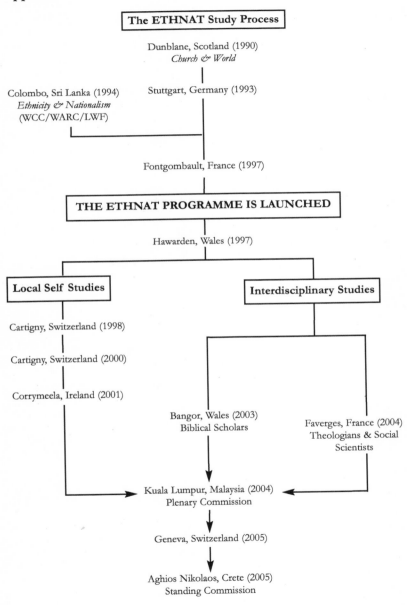

The ETHNAT Study Process

Dunblane, Scotland (1990)
Church & World

Colombo, Sri Lanka (1994)   Stuttgart, Germany (1993)
Ethnicity & Nationalism
(WCC/WARC/LWF)

Fontgombault, France (1997)

THE ETHNAT PROGRAMME IS LAUNCHED

Hawarden, Wales (1997)

Local Self Studies   Interdisciplinary Studies

Cartigny, Switzerland (1998)

Cartigny, Switzerland (2000)

Corrymeela, Ireland (2001)

Bangor, Wales (2003)   Faverges, France (2004)
Biblical Scholars   Theologians & Social
                               Scientists

Kuala Lumpur, Malaysia (2004)
Plenary Commission

Geneva, Switzerland (2005)

Aghios Nikolaos, Crete (2005)
Standing Commission